To order additional copies of this book, contact:
Xlibris
0800-056-3182
www.xlibrispublishing.co.uk
Orders@ Xlibrispublishing.co.uk

Life as Seen in the Eyes of Tatiana

Monica Brosnan

My name is Tatiana, and I was born into a human family's back garden, as was my brother Ginger. Ginger's name came from his colour. I am described as being tortoiseshell in colour. We began as animals in distress.

It was one of those days when anything that could go wrong had gone wrong. From day one, I had an ability to sniff trouble, and later on, this ability saved me. My pussycat mother had a lovely name, Abigail, and all who saw her agreed that she was truly beautiful. At times, people were cooing at her, giving her little goodie bags of snacks, and treating her like royalty.

We two kittens were usually hiding in the bushes, out of sight from everyone. From an early age, Ginger had a defiant streak that usually got him into trouble, and sometimes he was chastised by the owners of the family in whose garden we were born. The couple had no love for us kittens and would leave us out in the rain as we sheltered under shrubs, which eventually let the rain through.

These are vivid memories for me – and not happy ones. When I was nervous, I hissed at anyone who tried to lift me up. I had a plan to leap to the nearest shelter or squeeze between anything nearby where a human could not. Sometimes my terror intensified because I knew all about cats being put into cages.

On a happier note, when my mother arrived back, sometimes we would then be fed by her milk. She would keep us near her, and we three would be happy most nights. Whenever we were chased, Ginger's reaction was to lash out, fending off the attackers with a quick strike of his paw and an emphatic *eccow* noise with his teeth. I was usually a little shaken because fear travelled with me everywhere, even when I hid myself away and tried to sleep. Fear was my constant companion.

One day Abigail was present on such an occasion, and her reaction was to do something about our situation. She said, "This is our time."

We were now eight weeks old, and Ginger was by far the larger of us two. He was adopted by a new family who lived across the road. Then I was then taken by my mother, who carried me by grasping the back of my neck with her teeth. It was the time when the moon was our friend, and the humans were going to sleep. Moonlight seemed to me to be the friendliest time of all. Mother raced away down a road and jumped over a high wall while still holding on to me. I was nervous because everything was new to me.

On the other side of the wall was yet another very large garden and lots of shrubs. We hid once again under a bush. At this stage, I did not miss Ginger because he was becoming a little bully. Having my mother all on my own was very comforting, and I now felt safer in spite of the strange garden.

Next morning at daylight, as we awoke, we saw a house at the other end of our new garden. It is believed cats have nine lives. Was this my second? Cats are also curious and can be courageous, even at my tender age. We loved the moon that night but also welcomed daylight. I even stretched my paws out and yawned.

All day long, we were close together. Oh, what bliss! Suddenly there was a great noise as a tall man arrived on the lawn near us. He was pushing a gadget over the grass, and grass blades flew all over the place. We hid behind a bigger tree as we became more nervous. When he finished this job, he went away. I was not hungry in spite of not having eaten for two days.

The smell from somewhere was almost hypnotic. Curiosity from a safe spot under a bush was possible. We felt we were close to a human because we heard a voice whisper. My heart was pounding almost out of my body. I moved a paw and took a step, and my instincts were now powerful. The grass man we saw earlier was looking at us through the bush where we were hiding.

He moved a little closer and offered us a fish snack, which must have been where the lovely smell was coming from earlier. He left it on the ground, and Mother grabbed it between her teeth. She shared it with me and bit down on it ravenously while backing farther under the bush. This was almost heaven, and it was my first taste of a delicious snack. Mother was cleaning her whiskers, so I copied her.

Suddenly a hand grasped me, and I was lifted up. I raised my claws and mewed at him. Who was this grass man? I plunged my claws out and furiously scrabbled my back legs, dangling against his wrist. He laughed and lowered me a little while letting my legs hang. "Little one," he said, "no need to panic. I am not going to hurt you."

He rubbed the fur under my chin and then the top of my head. I liked that, in spite of my mother warning, "Never let a human hold you." I began to enjoy being cuddled, even though I had been kidnapped. I now felt quite assured that this man would not hurt me, and yet I was very small and almost alone with a human. I knew Mother was still nearby, and she was six months older than me and already out in the world.

I began to spend some time alone in my new garden when Mother was out hunting. The grass man would sometimes leave sardines for me on a saucer and move away without talking to me. Obviously he was using psychology on me until I might trust him. Other times he left a white liquid, and this quenched my thirst.

My kitten hood was improving for two reasons: the love of my mother and a new human friend who seemed to be nice. The moonlight became familiar, and I was beginning to stalk night insects in the light. Bats would also try to catch these insects.

Then came predawn, as the sun peeked over the horizon and the birds began to sing.

I tried to stalk the wildlife but was unsuccessful. A little later in life, I could not help but wonder how the little birds and little animals that I had stalked must have felt as I reflected on my own experiences with the grass man.

The itch to roam soon took precedence over my fear, which was now waning. I decided to venture out. In my short life, it was true I had not travelled far, and I would have to hop over many strange little barriers. The most frightening was trees, as any cat can tell you. Trees are ultimately deceptive and bewitching, and I found out as a kitten of eight weeks. A determined kitten can run up a tree in no time. My thoughts were, *but once there, is it impossible to get down? Can it be a claw-shredding, downwards scramble?*

Every cat likes a high place – as long as it is not up a tree. I was still my mother's kitten, and her words of advice made sense to me. I wished to return the friendship my new friend was extending to me and become the best kitten in the area. My ambition was to have a role in my new life.

I was quite hungry one day because the grass man had not appeared all day. Suddenly something moved in the grass. I sank down quietly, feeling my belly almost meld into the grass. I adjusted my position as my heart raced. There was no way for it to escape as I crouched. I eventually pounced and caught the animal. It was a shrew! It was so shocked it could not move, and I left it right there, feeling rather exhausted but proud of my new experience.

Darkness came, and I was still alone. Then morning came, and so did Mother. I related to her my story of what had happened over the previous twenty-four hours. She told me that a cat always should carry a catch as a trophy to show off to the people on whose premises one lives.

News of my first kill seemed to blow like a hurricane. I was now a heroine with my small circle of humans. But my companion of the last week was nowhere to be seen. It seemed that the grass man was done with me.

Mother, being anxious, carried me once again to the next-door garden. We arrived on a sunny morning. A tall man and a small lady saw us and tried to talk cat talk to us. Mother moved towards them on their balcony. I anxiously pondered them and stayed away; that was always Mother's advice. Little by little, despite the clamouring of my instincts, I began to get a sense that these two humans might not be so fearsome. Mother ate the food left nearby with hungry desperation. As soon as the two humans went inside, I joined Mother and ate a little of what remained.

My new human friends took care of us for many days. I tentatively and anxiously ran towards them when they left food on a saucer for us. I usually stood dithering and wondering if I should move close to these two humans, as Mother did.

Earlier in my kitten hood, I was taken to the veterinarian for an operation so that I could not have my own little family. My fur was taken off, and for some weeks I was always cold. I was registered as Jack, even though I was a girl kitten.

Ginger, my brother, turned into a monster and began beating me almost daily. Apparently neutered small kittens are a target for being bullied by bigger cats. I had not seen (or missed) Ginger for weeks. One day, he caught me and broke my front leg, which was put in a bandage at the clinic for small animals. I had to remain there for two days, and I was frightened and lonely. My only contact with my former life was to see the stars, which I knew were the same stars Mother viewed. I could look up and see the same sky. Otherwise, as a young kitten everything loomed rather threateningly, and there was nothing nice about it. I had to face up to others cats, and there were lots of confrontations in the cages around me.

When I arrived home, the two humans in my third home had made a home for me on their balcony, where I could sleep in comfort and no animal could reach me. Their names were Bill and Monica. To my great joy, there would be no more confrontations or fear. I supposed my new territory was for me alone to patrol. I would share my space only with these two humans forever willingly.

Then along came nasty Ginger one day as I sat alone in our large garden. I raced through the side entrance to the front garden. The huge tree at the end was my only hope of escape. I managed to climb it but was up there almost all day and night. There was no sign of Mother or the two humans.

Suddenly Monica began calling me by my new name, Tatiana. She coaxed me for a long time to come down, and Bill reached up the tree to help me down. It was much more difficult to climb down a tree than to go up; I was afraid I would fall down on my head. My confidence was returning with the tender loving care from my new landlords. The only confrontation from now on might be from my two human friends, but I was not certain I could trust them. Yet as a young kitten learning the ways of a cat, the world loomed rather threateningly. Having my own territory could involve lots of confrontations, facing up to cats with angry plans. This could involve a non-stop boundary patrol.

I loved my new human family and soon became happier than ever before. It became obvious that Monica and Bill loved me more than anything in the world. Even my personal hygiene was taken care of. I was now sharing my territory with two humans, but unfortunately they were not always at home.

Once again, terror struck when Ginger arrived, looking bigger and fatter than his last visit. I had been sleeping on a rug in my tiny house built specially for me so that I would be safe. Not being wise enough, I raced down the garden. Ginger followed me and mistreated me, and once again I was injured and in great pain. There was a great deal in life that I had yet to learn.

My new human family arrived home and called for me, but I could not move. I was the victim of yet another assault. This meant another visit to the clinic. I was not too nervous because my two human friends remained with me, and I was now familiar with the place. My curiosity got the better of me, and I listened carefully to the result of my X-ray. The result gave an extremely rude awakening to my human friends.

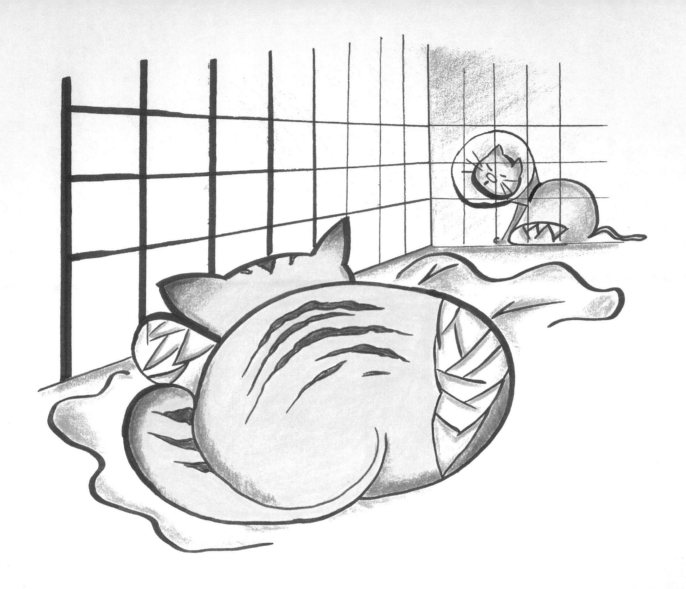

"I am sorry to say this, but we have to keep Tatiana for two days and nights. She has a pulled ligament."

I was in great pain, and trying to listen was not easy. I gave a loud meow for help. Then I was stuck with a needle and was in further pain. But soon my pain eased, and I felt very sleepy.

My life was one awful experience after another. There was no space – I was cooped up in a small cage and felt alone with fear and anxiety. Would I ever see my new human friends again? My nostrils were alert to the smell of big cats, which surrounded me from all sides in similar cages. It was all I could do to not panic. Then I heard what I thought were the voices of my two human friends. I was removed from the shelf where my cage was and taken to the reception area, where to my extreme delight, my human parents awaited me.

I was back out in my new home and out on the spacious lawn when my mother, Abigail, greeted me. Monica, my human mama, joined us, and we played together. Soon Monica produced a big plastic bag. We would jump into it as it was dragged around, as well as inside it; other times we simply followed it. I felt particularly full of myself and trotted along with a swagger, proud of myself for being surrounded by love. This garden became my favourite haunt, especially on warm, sunny days. When I was tired, I would curl up on the grass and sleep. Unlike me, Abigail seemed to revel in the fuss strangers made of her.

Time passed pleasantly, and I grew stronger. My beloved humans fussed over me, and this made me feel wanted and safe. They would say to me, "You felines are so supremely adaptable. You just get on with it." I loved it when they rubbed the cleft beneath my mouth and then smiled or took a few photos of me to show to family and friends.

I did not welcome strangers because there was no sure way of knowing how they might treat me. My parents would push these photos in my face and then nod towards me. "You know who that is, Tatiana?"

My human friends were decidedly cat lovers, and my life was happy. One afternoon, after having a lovely lunch of liver and nuts, I was taking a rest on a cushion. I was snapped out of my reverie when awful Ginger appeared. I raced towards the big tree at the end of the garden and managed to run up it. Out of nowhere came my human mama. She saw Ginger and chased him away, sprinkling him with water. He snapped back and refused to move, revealing his teeth. She picked up a brush and tried to shove him away, but he caught hold of it and refused to move, using bizarre behaviour and spewing angry noises. I watched as my nostrils and whiskers went into overdrive. I was still terrified and remained up the tree for many hours, until I was coaxed down by my human parents when they put a ladder against the tree and carried me down.

I was then taken into the sunroom in the family home by Monica, who believed that new rules had to be introduced for my safety. She had now spent one thousand Euros on my health and injuries. Prevention was the new rule of the day. I remained ever safe that night and slept beautifully. Bill had no experience with cats and was not keen to leave me in the house. Monica said she knew better because she'd had several cats in her lifetime that lived inside and lay on her bed at night. "They are among the cleanest animals known," she said.

Bill relented a little. "She must not go farther than the sunroom, and she should stay outside during the daytime."

"Okay, Bill." Monica set up my bed on a couch, and I spent the next year quite happy.

One day brazen Ginger sat by the couch because the door was open. Monica chased him away.

While in the clinic one day, I could not help thinking about what my mother had told me about bad luck, kittens, and cages. I supposed I was now officially leaving my kitten hood behind, and I stretched a little taller. It was quite a milestone. Cats are considered lucky, and most ship captains are happy to have a good luck cat on board, but they also are expected to earn their living by keeping rodents and cockroaches at bay. I am glad I was never chosen to go the seafaring way!

I was now safe and free in my permanent home with two loving humans and my own mother. I was never bored, and if ever I was strapped for entertainment, I simply chased my own tail. Bored took a great deal of fathoming and was beyond my comprehension. Some got down in the dumps; I believed this was a sister of being bored.

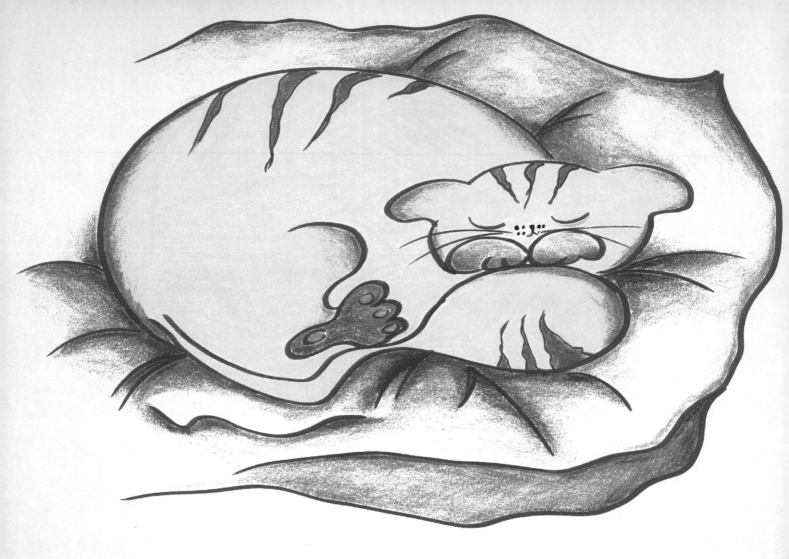

I had known the skirmishes that were the everyday part of animal nature, including the intent to kill. With these thoughts forgotten, I became mindful of my mother's words: "Never pass up an opportunity to have a nap." I took this advice whenever possible, especially after a meal of tender, barely cooked lamb liver. Vitamin E in liver did not agree with cats, and therefore it must be gently cooked.

During these naps, my mother visited me in my memories of happy times. We played on my lawn, often with my human family. They would drag a large plastic bag all over the grass, and we jumped into it and sometimes on top of it. This brought about shouts of joy and laughter. Following that, we two cats would be hoisted up in the air by our human friends.

For some days, Mother had not appeared, and Monica called and called for her. Mother often went on the busy road with human company for a walk. My bliss was soon shattered, and I felt traumatized because my sharp senses told me something was wrong. There was no news of Abigail.

I kept myself busy, and one day I pounced and caught a shrew in the long grass after a long struggle. To my delight, I later delivered my trophy to the humans' front door. I was exhausted, but it was a good kind of weariness, and the result of a job well done. I followed that with a wash, scrub, and clean.

An extraordinarily reward comes from living with an accommodating cat. Tatiana and I communicate with each other, and I interpret her language. She has a vocal personality, and her body language is subtle. It is easy to train her in spite of her sad upbringing and experiences. She retains a fear of people, but she's inveigled herself into my and Bill's life. Bill has never had a cat as a pet and was not keen to have her in our house. Within a year, he does not settle to sleep if Tatiana is not in our bedroom! She has also become very girly.

As I sit at my computer, she regularly jumps up on my desk, sits on my laptop as if to say, "Attention, please," and stares at me. She touches and smells everything in her reach. Her scent seems to be very sharp. She arches her back to let me know she is happy, but if she suspects danger, she also arches her back; in the latter case, her pupils dilate with fear. When I bring her to the vet, her pupils dilate due to her feeling threatened, and she will also pull her whiskers back along her cheeks. She is very aware of who is a cat lover and is more likely to socialize with that person. She can also be a drama queen when showing friendliness, rolling over, looking up, and inviting a belly rub.

Her language varies. A high-pitched meow means help. A more frantic one is a command: "Let me out to go to the toilet." High tones can also mean friendliness and happiness. Low tones can mean displeasure. Purring is peace and happiness, but apparently it can also mean comfort or pain.

I recently acquired new carpets in my home. This was bliss to Tatiana, and she delighted in sharpening her nails on my new stair carpet. I raised my voice when I caught her doing so. In a very short time, she picked up my vibe, and the habit was short-lived. I put a mat, cut from a leftover piece of my carpet, in front of her, and she has used that mat to sharpen her claws since. Her days and nights consist of many hours of sleeping, grooming, eating, and exploring. She lives willingly, happily, and contentedly with me. Her litter training came easily and quickly.

Her diet is drinking a lot of water and eating scientific nuts with all the trace elements her body requires. At least, my vet has told me so, adding that Tatiana should not grow fat on this diet. I also give her treats of fish and liver, both cooked lightly. In the summer she gets high on cat mint, a plant that dies down in winter. She eats it and rolls on it.

Tatiana never goes out on the street but views it from afar. For this I am very grateful because she is safe, and I am spared the worry; generally there is a great risk of cat injuries from road traffic. She no longer tries to catch birds but observes them very closely. She has the availability to eat meat without having to hunt for it. I read that experts say meat should be cooked because there is a risk of salmonella bacteria being picked up in raw poultry. I had toxoplasmosis when I was younger, caused by a parasite possibly from my cat. Humans pick up this parasite from poorly cooked meat. My cat can graze, which keeps the gums healthy.

I have always heard that cats have the power to heal and are intuitive when it comes to sniffing out illness in humans. One evening I went to bed early because I had a strong cough. Almost immediately Tatiana arrived on my bed and sat on my stomach. Obviously she'd detected something was wrong. I developed a bad cold and had difficulty shaking it off. I also read that in an old people's home in America, a resident cat became famous because she would sit with a resident who was in his or her final hours. Eventually people dreaded her cuddling up to them.

I have endless experiences with Tatiana's behaviour. For example, one sunny day she stayed outside in my garden from 8.00 a.m. until 6.00 p.m. I had left the house at approximately 6.00 p.m. and returned home at 11.15. Tracey, who was taking care of Tatiana, tried to entice her inside several times. As always, she was worried that Tatiana would not come into the house.

Tracey greeted me on arrival, quite worried. I went to the garden balcony, and immediately Tatiana rushed in and up to my bed. Like a naughty child, she was not happy that I had gone out. Her purring hit the roof, and she slept well that night.

Tatiana decided one day that she had earned her living and done a really good day's work. The sun was like a blanket on her back as she watched the birds flying and landing nearby. This was frustrating for little Tatiana. I could imagine her thinking, "Why are they not coming closer to me?"

Suddenly, she successfully captured a large mouse and presented the trophy to me as I sat on my balcony. She was puffed with pride and strode off. Then she jumped into her comfortable bed nearby, settled down, and kneaded the smooth cushion under her as she settled into her comfort zone. I produced some food for her, and with a thrill of excitement, she leapt from her bed. She didn't hesitate in tackling her food without her usual stretching act. It was already evening, and the sky was turning a peachy pink; the temperature had grown warmer. I then took my little princess inside to the security of our bed.

I was quite sad about the presentation from Tatiana earlier in the evening, in spite of knowing the nature of cats. When they hunt and catch birds, it is usually an already weakened one.

I am so proud to be in the same league with such a famous man as Mark Twain, who said, "When a man loves cats, I am his friend and comrade without further introduction."

I enjoy getting to know what cats are thinking. We ought to enjoy cats' company by pretending that they are also little people. I greatly appreciate being able to share my life with Tatiana, my enigmatic companion with a child-like face and eyes. I have raised her to iconic status. I have been fascinated with cats since I was a child. One cat shared my bicycle journeys with me, and she sat on my shoulder over long journeys. My dear late mama shared my love of all animals. Having studied bio-medical science (science of the human body), I have at times reflected on how it would be to study feline science, as many famous people have.

I will reveal how I was thinking as a kitten. Consequently, those thoughts constructed my version of the world. I gathered information about my surroundings. My hypersensitive sense of smell led my brain to interpret information. I experienced fear at an early age. My friendship with humans did not come easy, as it was with cats millions of years ago. Monica is the object of my affection, and ever since my kitten days, I've trusted her completely.

My brother, Ginger, had ginger fur. That colour is inherited from special chromosomes in male cats, according to Monica. He was different from me in every way. She also told me that my tabby pattern inherited one gene from the mother and one from the father. It's thought to be ideal camouflage.

Tatiana will reveal some of my thoughts and feelings. I do have quite a nervous disposition. I still remember when I was a kitten, and if a human unknown to be approached, I would patrol the house to find a hiding place. At times humans would try to come close to me if they found my hiding place, when Mother wished to show me off because she was very proud of me. I know I am like Cassius Clay: pretty! I then was forced to hide yet again. Minutes after strangers left our house, I would bond immediately with Mother and shed the stress.

My personality was learnt as a kitten. My world was an endless effort to fend for myself. I was neutered and small, which meant I was a receipt of being bullied.

Fortunately, in my garden there was only one enemy, my brother. Ginger was large and vicious. Luckily, after having spent a lot of my kitten days running up a large tree, I became an expert at dashing up trees without being followed. Ginger even scratched some local humans.

I had no friends of my own except my human mother. To attract her attention, I would roll over on my back, belly up, to entice her to play with me. I only wished to be with the few I was well acquainted with. I was not capable of multiple socialization due to what I had to contend with as a kitten and later as a juvenile.

I never feel my abilities as inferior. I was good at being a cat. We cats have lived alongside humans for over four thousand years. Yet I believe our senses differ, or even complement each other. We are both mammals.

I can see with my great big green eyes, but I am not a monster with big green eyes! I can see better in the darkness because my pupils expand much greater than humans do. Experts who have studied cats maintain the sensitivity of my eyes and cats in general is enhanced up to 40 per cent

Humans can see better than me in daylight. Again, the experts remind me that cats have difficulty distinguishing colours, but so do some humans who are colour-blind. My ears stand erect at times of fear and also when going through long grass or shrubs, especially when I hear a rustle in the growth. My hearing is superior to humans due to my pinnate, which is the visible part of my ears. My dainty paws are very sensitive, and I hate to have them touched due to the many nerve endings.

I was amazed Tatiana bothered hunting because she has always had a balanced diet, and the quality of a cat's diet affects its desire to hunt. Cats are carnivores, and if they're fed on household scraps high in carbohydrates, it can give them a craving for protein food – meat. Therefore cats on a poor diet will be hunters through nutritional necessity.

At dusk when I often let Tatiana out in my garden, especially in monsoon-type weather, it is almost impossible to coax her inside. The damp, moist weather attracts insects in great numbers. She ignores me as I call her and continues pouncing and stalking the insects in the air until she loses interest.

Nervous cats often prefer to rub themselves on an object such as a chair or the edge of a table, instead of on their owner, if they do not know the people present. They will rub on their owner's leg, confirming their confidence. Tatiana mostly rubs on objects in spite of our closeness, perhaps it comes from her unhappy kitten hood. I understand these actions have a lot to do with the scent from the glands on the side of cats' heads being deposited, marking an object.

Tatiana has many forms of greeting. She uses purring to coax me to do something for her. A loud meow is her method of attracting my attention. She'll jump on to my lap to remind me to let her out. A brief chirrup in passing is to say hello. Some meows are urgent and very demanding. Of course, I too have my cat chat that she understands, and hence she can judge my moods. If I raise my voice when she is sharpening her paws on my new carpets, she grows very nervous and runs away for a while. She learned very quickly to sharpen her paws only on the mat provided. I believe that she is very intelligent.

I do not wish to travel outside Ireland presently; anyhow, I have been to all seven continents and am happy to avoid awful travel conditions. When I do take a few days' break, I am anxious to be reunited with Tatiana because she has few people she feels are decent and whom she allows embrace her. This lack of trust reverts back to her sad kitten hood when, on many occasions, an aggressive male cat lunged at her. To this day, if another cat arrives in our garden, she freaks out and makes a loud yowling noise to draw my attention to the situation. Yet each evening close to dusk, I feed our visiting fox. Tatiana waits for a long time each evening, watching for the fox's arrival on the lawn as she sits in comfort from her cosy cat seat in our lounge. One day she walked down the lawn side by side with the fox. Normally in such cases, the cat is the boss, and she is quicker in retort if necessary.

There is a phrase that goes, "A cat will be your friend but will never be your slave." Cats will never be with someone they do not wish to be with, and they are never going to do something they don't want to do. Certainly Tatiana has a very strong character with a free will of her own. I have read a book written by a down-and-out in London, and he became a multimillionaire following the successful book he wrote about his cat Bob. He reckons cats have the power to heal bones with their purring; it's something to do with the frequency at which they vibrate that somehow strengthen the bones.

I do not wish to travel much with the exception of breaks of no more than four days. First and foremost, I would miss my darling Tatiana. Second, the crush in airports does not appeal to me. In days gone by, when travel was restricted to the few, it was also a luxury because during the flight, one was treated to a four-course, high-class meal. I have been to the seven continents and almost everywhere in the world more than once. Tatiana remains an extremely nervous cat, no doubt due to her sad kitten hood when the odd larger male cat lunges at her. More often than not, she escaped up a tree; this speed to get away was nurtured out of necessity.

I acquired a new pet over the past five years: a fox which I feed nightly. Presently, she has three adorable cubs. Tatiana has no problem with her because as in all cases, apparently the cat is the boss in such circumstances. I believe it is not possible to tame these beautiful creatures.

I treat Tatiana as a human and have lots of chats with her. In fact, one of the pleasures of owning a cat as a pet and companion is projecting feelings and thoughts to them. Apparently biologists refer to cats and other animals that mentally process information as having cognition; there is not enough room in their brains to pick up all the information their sense organs process. Yet Tatiana has experienced rough times in her early life, as do some children, and emotionally both must remember.

My cat dictates where she wishes to be touched, and she will not allow stroking past her neck. She demonstrates her appreciation of our bonding by holding her tail upright. I had the great pleasure of living for fifteen years in Switzerland, which is unique in the world. Thank God for their four distinctive seasons, all of which are truly superb. There's been no war in eight hundred years, transportation runs like clockwork, and it's almost devoid of violence because penalties are very harsh, and therefore it is too big a risk.

A person who wishes to adopt a cat or dog will have the appropriate authorities check the home, interview those involved, set out a strict list of care for the animal, and follow up annually. Tatiana is a modern girl and is micro chipped, and hence she can be located by the police if she's lost because computer data can reveal details.

It is unlikely I shall have this problem because she stays within my property and views traffic, birds, and humans from a distance, enjoying her contentment. When playing, she tumbles into a heap and waits for me to take her in my arms.

I do not need an alarm because Tatiana wakes up when she is ready, moves closer to my face, and stares for some minutes. Sooner or later, a gentle paw will stroke my face to remind me to get up. At times if I am awake before her, I pretend to be asleep and enjoy the whole scene. Her breakfast of a small helping of organic egg flip with added medication of Arthriaid (to prevent rheumatism later due to her injuries as a kitten) and liquid Paraffin (to keep her healthy), plus a tiny piece of garlic in her food. That's followed by a fistful of scientific nuts containing all the trace elements. Each January she has a complete check-up, and monthly I apply special drops to prevent her from picking up anything that might affect her. She also receives a special injection twice annually.

My greatest pleasure is seeing her get tipsy when she eats catnip, followed by face rubbing and leading into ecstatic body rolling. I am informed that the Japanese cat shrub has a similar effect. Cats' sense of smell has evolved for socializing as well as hunting. Tatiana demonstrates this to me at certain times. For example, she can detect a visitor to my home before I do by sniffing. She has quite an arsenal at her disposal, and she approaches silently and stealthily if there is even suspicion of prey nearby, her whiskers on her face sweeping forward.

Climbing a tree is not a normal venture for her unless necessary, because coming down is difficult. Cat claws all face forward and cannot be used as brakes when descending. Her routine has a daily rhythm. She seems to take cues from the environment. For example, by the onset of daylight, her breakfast meal, which is roughly the same time each morning, is followed by a stroll down the garden path. Halfway down, she stops at exactly the same place, a tree, and scans the house to see if I am coming too. She will not move until I join her. The tree where she stops is given a quick inspection, perhaps revealing an odour indicating that another mammal has visited.

Sometime later, I will inform her that I am present and clap my hands to announce myself. I taught her this habit as a kitten. I have learnt that there are many ways of training a cat, such as using a clicker followed by food rewards. Her tail in the air when approaching me means she wants to be friendly or wishes to go to the toilet. On meeting another cat, she will bluff and draw herself up to full height, turn partially sideways, and put her ears backwards in case there is a fight. Failing all of that, she snarls.

The End

CPSIA information can be obtained at www.ICGtesting.com
Printed in the USA
LVIW01n1432020817
543566LV00009B/81

9 781524 594503